"Gwen Costello has written many books of p[   ]
teenagers. Now she has turned her attention to th[   ]
vided them with a welcome and affirming resourc[   ] prayer ser-
vices, organized around the school year, offer catechists time to gather and reflect, to
refresh and renew themselves, and to get a large dose of new conviction and commitment. Catechist and teacher meetings are sure to reach new levels of shared
insight and deeper prayer with these thoughtful services."

Deborah McCann
Columnist, *Religion Teachers Journal*

"This is more than a book of prayer services. It is a book of prayer experiences that
will empower DREs and school principals to help their staffs share their faith in
practical, meaningful ways. This book will be a welcome resource through all the
seasons of the year. It will be a model of simple faith sharing and the use of Scripture
and personal stories so that teachers, in turn, can learn to lead students in prayer."

Peg Bowman
Director of Catechesis
Diocese of Rockford, IL

"My experience in religious education has taught me that catechists hunger for the
opportunity to come together spiritually. As much as I want to provide opportuni-
ties for spiritual development, I quickly exhaust my files. Gwen's book supplies catechetical leaders with prayer experiences that focus on a wide variety of themes.
The brief prayer services allow for all participants to collect spirit and mind in God's
presence before going about the task of their gathering."

Marianne Slattery, DRE
St. Noel Parish
Willoughby Hills, OH

"The best thing about *Prayer Services for Catechist and Teacher Meetings* is that Gwen
Costello provides prayer experiences that involve much more than just words. They
include the use of symbols, gestures, movement, silence, shared prayer, and more.
If we are trying to teach our children that prayer is more than just 'talking to God,'
we should encourage catechists to pray in a manner that engages all their senses.
Costello has created a valuable resource for DREs to enrich the prayer experiences
of their catechists. I intend to use these at my catechist meetings!"

Joe Paprocki
Pastoral Associate and DRE
Author and host, *Empowering the Catechist* (video)

"Gwen Costello knows how to get to the heart of the matter. Her *Prayer Services for
Catechist and Teacher Meetings* are topical, practical, and do-able for a busy DRE or
principal. Each theme uses related symbols, scripture passages, and ritual actions to
expand a kernel of wisdom into a time of reflection and personal involvement that
focuses on the catechetical dimension of the participants' ministry. I adapted one of
the prayer services for a year-end catechist gathering and it was a most meaningful
experience."

Marilyn Peters Krawczyk
Director of Religious Education
Holy Cross Parish, Deerfield, IL

GWEN COSTELLO

PRAYER SERVICES

for Catechist & Teacher Meetings

TWENTY-THIRD PUBLICATIONS

Mystic, CT 06355

Twenty-Third Publications
185 Willow Street
P.O. Box 180
Mystic, CT 06355
(860) 536-2611
800-321-0411

ISBN 0-89622-696-4
Library of Congress Catalog Card Number 96-60347
Printed in the U.S.A.

Contents

Introduction

This is a resource for proclaimers, particularly for religion teachers and catechists, including RCIA catechists, who have accepted the call to share their faith. An important, even essential, aspect of Christian proclamation is prayer. We share faith as much through our expression of it in prayer as through what we say "about" it—maybe even more so. When we can combine the two, when our prayer also teaches us something about our faith, we are doubly blessed.

The services in this book are an attempt to offer "double blessings." They offer complete prayer experiences that also teach valuable faith lessons. In every case participants are involved in some manner so that they can respond to God in realistic, practical ways. Prayer is a real experience that relates to our lives here and now. God exists and reaches out to us. God is with us in all our life experiences. We reach back toward God when we share this belief with one another and express it through prayer.

All of this applies in double measure when proclaimers gather to pray. When our catechists and teachers of the faith can experience God as real and present, they will more convincingly pass this truth on and celebrate it with those they teach. These services, while for the proclaimers themselves, will ultimately benefit every child, teenager, and RCIA candidate whose lives they touch.

Use these services often, every time you gather to prepare for or to sustain your ministry. Adapt them to your own particular group and situations. Let them inspire you to develop your own, highly personal, prayer services. Involve all participants in creating words and rituals that express the process of learning about and responding to God as your group experiences it. It doesn't really matter which words and rituals you use; the important thing is to pray together often. My hope is that these services will be a starting point as you continue to support one another in your proclamation of God's presence in your midst.

We Are Bearers of Truth

To Prepare

Place on your prayer table a bible (open to John 17), a lighted candle, and any symbols that represent the teachings of the church, for example: the documents of Vatican II, the *Catechism of the Catholic Church,* a textbook, a teacher's manual, a lectionary. Beforehand, make copies of the following "Prayer for Catechists" for distribution at the end of the service:

Loving God, you have called me to proclaim your Word. I want to respond generously, but I feel so inadequate, so unsure of myself. I don't have all the answers. Teach me to rely on your wisdom, to believe that you are there in every class I teach. Help me to understand that you can and do touch the minds and hearts of your children—through me. Above all, make me wise enough to trust that the seeds of faith I have sown—with your help—will someday blossom and grow in your children. Amen.

Leader	May the Spirit of Truth and Wisdom dwell with you and be in your hearts. May the Spirit be with you in all that you do to proclaim God's Word.
All	And also with you.
Leader	We are gathered here, God of Truth and Wisdom, to ask your blessing on us as we begin a new teaching year. Open our minds to your wisdom, truth, and goodness that we might share these gifts with your children.
Reader One	At the Last Supper, Jesus prayed this prayer in the presence of his disciples: "This is eternal life, that they may know you, the only true God, and Jesus Christ whom you have sent."
All	Help us to know you, God our God.
Reader Two	Jesus continued, "I have made your name known to those you gave me. They were yours, and you gave them to me, and they have kept your Word…They know in truth that I came from you."
All	Help us to make your name known, God our God.
Reader Three	Then Jesus said, "Sanctify them in the truth; your word is truth. As you have sent me into the world, so I have sent them into the world.

	And for their sakes I sanctify myself, so that they also may be sanctified in truth."
All	Bless us with your truth, God our God.
Reader Four	Finally, Jesus prayed, "I ask not only on behalf of these here with me now, but also on behalf of those who will come to believe in me through their word, that they may all be one. As you, Father, are in me and I am in you, may they also be in us, so that the world may believe that you have sent me."
All	Give us faith in Jesus Christ, God our God.
Leader	This prayer of Jesus contains the following central teachings of our Catholic Christian faith:
Reader One	God is the true God who sent Jesus Christ to dwell among us.
Reader Two	Jesus made God's name known, and he shared the truth of God's kingdom.
Reader Three	God's Word is truth. Jesus wants his followers to be steeped in truth.
Reader Four	It is our faith in God that unites us, and we have been called to share this faith with those we teach.
Leader	Let us now take time for silent prayer to reflect on the words of Jesus and to discern how we might live out the truth and wisdom they proclaim.
	Allow three minutes or so for silent reflection.
Leader	Be with us God of all truth and wisdom as we struggle this year to share your word with our children and teenagers.
Right Side	Help us to be witnesses of faith who give example to those we teach.
Left Side	Give us patience, love, and most of all courage to wisely proclaim your truth.
Leader	I invite you to come forward to receive a reminder that you can and should rely on God's guidance this year in every class you teach.
	As you give each catechist a prayer card, say: "_____, *let this prayer remind you of your call to be a catechist." When all have received their cards, share a greeting of peace with one another.*

2

We Rejoice in Our Faith

To Prepare

In your prayer space place a lighted candle, a bible (open to Ephesians 1:15–23), a textbook, and a teacher's manual. Beforehand, write out or type onto slips of paper lines from the following service. For example: "May you understand the great power you have received," or, "May God give you the spirit of wisdom." Place these "blessing" slips in a container on your prayer table.

Leader	It is with God's own power that we are called forth as teachers and catechists. It is only with God's gifts of wisdom, revelation, and mercy that we can serve, as the following reading proclaims.
Reader One	A reading from Ephesians: "Ever since I heard about your faith, I have not stopped giving thanks for you and remembering you in my prayers. I keep asking God to give you the spirit of wisdom and revelation, so that you may know God better.
Reader Two	"I pray also that the eyes of your heart may see what it is God is calling you to. And may you see the glorious inheritance that is planned for you and understand the great power you have received.
Reader Three	"This power is the same power that God used to raise Jesus from the dead and to place him above all created things. With Christ, we can now experience the fullness of God who fills up everything in every way." The Word of the Lord.
All	Thanks be to God.
Leader	(holding up the candle from the prayer table) See this light, a symbol of Christ. May the light of Christ fill your minds and hearts as you prepare to serve the church.
All	We welcome the light of Christ.
Leader	(holding up the bible) See this book that contains the Word of God. May you share its wisdom and revelation with those you serve.

All	We welcome the Word of God.
Leader	(holding up the textbook) See this textbook that contains a message of faith. May you guide each person who uses it to a greater knowledge and love of God.
All	We welcome this message of faith.
	Now pick up the "blessing" slips from the table and invite each person to come forward to take one. When all have them in hand, invite catechists to offer the blessing on the slip to at least two others in the room. Encourage them to extend a hand toward the person they are blessing. Allow sufficient time for this.
Leader	I invite you now to spend time in silence asking God for particular blessings that you might need.
	Allow three minutes or so for this.
Leader	For each of you, that you may understand your calling, experience the power of God, and appreciate your gifts. Let us pray to the Lord…
All	Lord, hear our prayer.
	Add several petitions that apply directly to all present, and then invite participants to pray their own spontaneous prayers. When all have prayed, conclude as below.
Leader	God, our loving parent, guide and strengthen us, and above all, calm our fears as we go forth to proclaim the gospel. Watch over us and bless us always.
All	Amen.

3

Jesus Is Always Near

To Prepare

Place the following objects on your prayer table: a white candle, a bible (open to Psalm 145), a textbook, and a teacher's manual. Optional: If possible, also have on the table a small object for each participant, some small reminder of their role as proclaimers. Examples include verse or holy cards, bookmarks, and pins.

Leader   Great is our God and worthy of all praise. Together let us acclaim God who offers us love and compassion as we begin this new teaching year.

Reader One   (adapted from Psalm 145): Gracious God, you are faithful in all your words, and holy in all your works. You lift up all who are falling and raise up all who are bowed down.

Reader Two   The eyes of all look hopefully to you, and you give them bread in due season. You open your hand and satisfy the desire of every living thing.

Reader Three   Gracious God, you are just in all your ways and loving in all your works. You are near to all who call upon you, to all who call upon you sincerely.

Reader Four   You fulfill the desire of those who fear you, you hear their cry and save them. You watch over all who love you.

Leader   We acknowledge that as we begin this new year, we are in need of God's love and compassion. God offers this to us through Jesus. We recognize how much we need Jesus near us, to hear our calls for help and guidance. We are teachers and proclaimers, called to be models for those we serve, but we recognize our weakness. Together let us ask Jesus for guidance as we begin anew.

Reader Five   At those times when we will feel impatient, unprepared, harried, or put upon...

All   Be near us, Jesus.

Reader Six	At those times when we forget to pray, ignore your presence, or proclaim your Word poorly…
All	Be near us, Jesus.
Reader Seven	At those times when we are not just in all our ways, or loving in all our works…
All	Be near us, Jesus.
Reader Eight	At those times when we fail to give joyful witness to you and to your love and compassion…
All	Be near us, Jesus.
Leader	I invite you now to spend a few moments in quiet reflection about the challenges and joys that await you and your class this year. In particular, pray for those you will be teaching.
	Allow five minutes for this and if possible play soft background music.
Leader	Gracious God, you lift up those who are falling and you raise up all who are bowed down. You are near to all who call upon you, to all who call upon you sincerely. You are present to us through Jesus, your son, in whose name we now pray.
All	Jesus, as we begin this new teaching year, we know that we need your love and compassion. We recognize how much we need you near us, to help us and guide us. We are teachers and proclaimers of your presence among us, but we can't proclaim without your help. Be with us, please, now and always. Amen.
	Optional: Now call each catechist forward by name and present her or him with the small gift from your prayer table. As you present these say, "_____, may this be a reminder to you that Jesus is always near."

4

God Gives Us Gifts

> **To Prepare**
> On your prayer table place a bible open to 1 Corinthians 16:13, a lighted candle, and any symbols that represent proclaiming faith for your group, for example, a textbook and manual or a crucifix. Also have available slips of paper, one for each participant, on which one of these four words is written: Awareness, Courage, Strength, Love. Place these slips in a basket on your prayer table.

Leader   God, our God, you are gracious and generous beyond our wildest imaginings. You have visited us and left us the gift of your presence. Teach us to respond to this precious gift with deep faith, now and always.

All   Amen.

Reader One   In Paul's first letter to the Christians at Corinth, he offers a very brief and to-the-point message, one that is very appropriate for us as we gather now to study our faith and to be strengthened by one another's faith.

Reader Two   Keep alert!

All   Help us to keep alert, gracious God.

Reader Three   Stand firm in your faith!

All   Teach us to stand firm in our faith, loving God.

Reader Four   Be courageous!

All   Strengthen us to be courageous, sustaining God.

Reader Two   Be strong!

All   Show us how to be strong, giver of all good gifts.

Reader Three   Let all that you do be done in love.

All	Let all that we do be done in love, gracious and generous God.
Leader	This brief reading describes four of the gifts we need to be people of faith: awareness, courage, moral strength, and above all, love. Which of these gifts do you possess? Which do you long for?
	Pick up the basket from your prayer table.
	I invite you to come forward now and take one of these papers. Then spend a few moments prayerfully reflecting on the word written on it.
	Allow at least three minutes for this.
Reader One	God of Awareness, teach us what it means to be alert, open, waiting for your presence. Let us be aware of you always.
Reader Two	God of Courage, forgive us for the times we have been faithless and afraid. Renew us and make us courageous witnesses.
Reader Three	God of Strength, share this great gift with us, for we are so often weak. Make our faith strong and true that we might proclaim it to our children.
Reader Four	God of Love, pour your abundant love into us that we might welcome and embrace all of your children as you welcome and embrace us.
Leader	God our God, you are gracious and generous beyond our wildest imaginings. You have visited us and left us the gift of your presence. Teach us to respond to this precious gift with deep faith, now and always.
All	Amen.

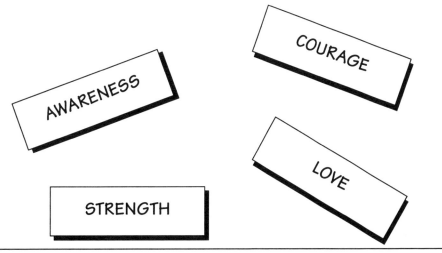

We Are Called to Be Saints

To Prepare

Place on your prayer table a bible (open to Acts 20:17–24), a lighted candle, and any objects that symbolize our call to holiness, including books, videos, or other resources about saints.

Leader	Holy, holy, holy, Lord God of Hosts, heaven and earth are filled with your glory. Hosanna in the highest.
All	Blessed is he who comes in the name of the Lord. Hosanna in the highest.
Leader	Jesus is the blessed one who dwells among us. Those who take their faith and their relationship with God very seriously, so seriously that they feel compelled to share what they have discovered, are called saints. Our world today is badly in need of saints who will proclaim to our children the message of the gospel and who will dedicate their lives to this task. We need people like the apostle Paul who wrote the following:
Reader One	"I'm sure you know how I have lived among you ever since I first set foot in Asia. You know how I have served the Lord most humbly and what tears I have shed over the trials that have come to me…
Reader Two	"You know that I have never held back from telling you anything that was for your good, nor from teaching you in public or in your own homes. On the contrary, I have most emphatically urged upon you repentance toward God and faith in our Lord Jesus.
Reader Three	"And now, here I am, compelled by the Spirit to go to Jerusalem. I don't know what may happen to me there, except that the Holy Spirit warns me that persecution awaits me. But frankly, I don't consider my own life valuable to me unless I can complete the ministry which the Lord Jesus has given me in declaring the good news of the grace of God." The Word of the Lord.
All	Thanks be to God.
Leader	It's hard for us to imagine that anyone would risk his or her life to proclaim the gospel. Fortunately for us, proclaiming the good news

today is not a life-threatening ministry. And yet, in a way it is.

Reader Four   For the gospel message of Jesus threatens our "way of life." It warns us not to put our hope in material things, but rather in God. It teaches us that we must love one another and care for one another, and that we must share our resources.

Leader   This is hardly a message people want to hear. And yet we are called to proclaim it. Let us now, each in his or her own heart, pray for the grace and the strength to live the gospel and proclaim it.

Allow five minutes for this.

Leader   Let us pray now for our own needs as disciples and for the needs of those we teach.

Reader One   That we might never shrink from telling our children the true message of the gospel, let us pray to the Lord…

All   Lord, hear our prayer.

Reader Two   That we might constantly urge those we teach to repentance and faith in our Lord Jesus, let us pray to the Lord…

All   Lord, hear our prayer.

Reader Three   That we might always declare the good news of the grace of God, let us pray to the Lord…

All   Lord, hear our prayer.

Leader   I invite you now to add your own intentions…

All   Lord, hear our prayer.

After the petitions, ask each person to turn to the person on his or her right and share with that person one insight he or she has gained from this prayer time. After the sharing, invite all to pray silently for the person with whom the sharing was done. Allow two minutes or so for this.

Leader   Let us pray. Help us, Lord Christ, to be courageous in our proclamation of the gospel—as Paul was, as all of your saints were. We ask this in the name of the Father, and of the Son, and of the Holy Spirit.

All   Amen.

If you have placed "saint" items on your prayer table, invite catechists to look at them before they leave. Encourage them to borrow any of the books or videos you may have displayed.

We Are God's Proclaimers

> **To Prepare**
> Place on your prayer table a bible (open to Matthew 5:1–13) and a candle.

Leader   We are gathered here in the presence of God and one another to reflect on our role as catechists and teachers. Together we will seek guidance from Jesus in whose name we have accepted the call to proclaim God's Word. When the disciples asked Jesus where he lived, he answered, "Come and see." And they went with him and spent the day with him. Let us, too, "come and see" where Jesus lives and let us now spend time in his presence.

Allow five minutes or so for silent prayer and reflection.

Reader One   A reading from the Gospel of Matthew:
"Jesus saw the people and went up a hill, where he sat down. His disciples gathered around him and he began to teach them: Happy are those who know they are spiritually poor; the kingdom of heaven belongs to them. Happy are those who mourn; God will comfort them.

Reader Two   "Happy are those who are humble; they will receive what God has promised. Happy are those whose greatest desire is to do what God asks; God will satisfy them fully. Happy are those who show mercy to others; God will be merciful to them.

Reader Three   "Happy are the pure in heart; they will see God. Happy are those who work for peace; they will be called the children of God. Happy are those who are persecuted because they do what God requires; to them, too, the kingdom of heaven belongs."
The Word of the Lord.

All   Thanks be to God.

Leader	No doubt in the quiet of your hearts Jesus spoke to you and you to him. And in the scripture we have just heard, Jesus speaks to us about the qualities he hopes to see in us and in all those who follow him. He asks us to recognize our poverty, to console the sorrowing, to be humble, to seek God's will, to show mercy, to be single-minded, and to work for peace. But Jesus asks even more.
Reader Four	"You are the salt of the earth," Jesus said, "but if salt loses its flavor, what good is it? It can only be thrown out. You are the light of the world. People don't light candles and then hide them under bushel baskets. Rather, they put them in candlesticks so they can give light to everyone in the house. Let your light shine in such a way that people everywhere can see your good works and give glory to your Father in heaven."
Leader	We have heard the words of Jesus, and he challenges us in our task as catechists, as proclaimers of God's Word. Let us now pray together for the gifts we need to accomplish this great work.
Right Side	Teach us to be all that we can be, Jesus; teach us to be salt for the earth and light for the world.
Left Side	Show us how to do only good works, Jesus, in our homes, in our classes, and in our workplaces.
Right Side	Teach us in all that we do, Jesus, in all our words and actions, to give glory to our Father in Heaven.
	Invite catechists to add spontaneous requests they may have.
Leader	Jesus, present with us, help us to understand what you are asking of us as proclaimers of your Word. Guide us in all our efforts with those we teach.
All	Amen.

7
We Thank God Always

<table>
<tr><td colspan="2">To Prepare
Make a banner or large poster with these words on it: I THANK MY GOD FOR YOU. Hang it in a visible place. On your prayer table, place a bible (open to Philippians 1:3–6) and a candle.</td></tr>
</table>

Reader One   The Lord Jesus Christ be with you.

All   And also with you.

Leader   Believing that Jesus is indeed with us, let us listen to God's Word, which reminds us of the gifts we have received.

Reader One   A reading from Paul's letter to the Christians at Philippi:
"I thank my God for each of you whenever I think of you. My constant prayers for you are a real joy, for they bring to mind how we have worked together for the gospel from the earliest days until now. I feel sure that the one who has begun this good work in you will go on developing it, until the day when Jesus comes again in glory."
The Word of the Lord.

All   Thanks be to God.

Reader Two   God has given us an amazing variety of gifts for which to give thanks: the created world with all its mysterious cycles and changes; natural wonders like waterfalls and rainbows; flowers in spring, the summer sun, glorious colors in the fall, the calm, cold quiet of winter.

Reader Three   God has given us our bodies and our minds: our hands and feet to do our bidding; our lips to smile and our ears to hear; our mouths with which to communicate and to enjoy food and drink.

Reader Four   God has given us a human spirit that neither the created world nor our bodies can contain: a spirit that composes music and poetry; a courageous spirit that serves those in need; a spirit that ultimately overcomes evil with good; a spirit that never gives up its search for meaning and truth.

Reader Five   God has given us other people: spouses and children, family and friends, coworkers and those with whom we minister; unique people, none of whom are exactly the same; people who sometimes give us joy, sometimes burden us; people who love and care for us unconditionally; people who need us and depend on us.

Leader   Let us pause now to reflect on one personal talent, or one gift of nature, or one special person for whom we feel particularly grateful at this moment.

Allow two minutes for this.

Leader   Of all God's created gifts, Paul recognized that people were among the greatest.

Let us now pray together spontaneous prayers of thanksgiving for the people who are dearest to our hearts.

Begin these thanksgiving invocations yourself in this way:

For all the catechists of this parish, who support and encourage me in my work for the gospel, I offer thanks to God…

All   We thank you and praise you, great God.

When all have had the opportunity to offer their prayers of thanks, invite catechists to bless one another using Paul's words. Ask the person nearest you to begin by turning to the person on his or her right and offering this blessing: "_____, may God continue to work in you." The person should answer "Amen." When the blessing comes full circle, join hands and recite the following closing prayer:

All   Glory be to the Father, and to the Son, and to the Holy Spirit, as it was in the beginning, is now, and ever shall be, world without end. Amen.

I THANK MY GOD FOR YOU

8

We Share the Gift of Waiting

> **To Prepare**
>
> Place on your prayer table a bible (open to 1 Corinthians 16:13–14), a candle, and a container that holds copies of the following prayer refrain from the Scripture cited above: "Give us the gift of waiting, loving God. Help us to keep alert, to stand firm in our faith, to be courageous and strong. Let all that we do be done in love."

Leader   Advent is a time for waiting. We await the feast of Christmas when we will celebrate the birth of Jesus Christ. But Advent is also a time to look at waiting in an entirely new way. Waiting can also mean *being present and open* to how Jesus is among us right now: in our encounters with others, in our daily tasks, in our teaching, in our enjoyment of a beautiful day, in our prayer, in our worship, and so on.

This kind of waiting is like opening our eyes to what *already is* and *being alert* to God's every epiphany. Let us pray for this gift of waiting.

All   Give us the gift of waiting, loving God. Help us to keep alert, to stand firm in our faith, to be courageous and strong. Let all that we do be done in love.

Reader One   Help us to see your presence in every child we teach and to love and respect each child as a unique and treasured person.

All   Give us the gift of waiting, loving God. Help us to keep alert, to stand firm in our faith, to be courageous and strong. Let all that we do be done in love.

Reader Two   Help us to prepare every lesson we teach carefully, remembering that we are proclaiming your Word and your presence.

All   Give us the gift of waiting, loving God. Help us to keep alert, to

	stand firm in our faith, to be courageous and strong. Let all that we do be done in love.
Reader One	Help us seek out quiet time this Advent, time when we can peacefully place ourselves in your hands and hold out to you the children we teach.
All	Give us the gift of waiting, loving God. Help us to keep alert, to stand firm in our faith, to be courageous and strong. Let all that we do be done in love.
Reader Two	Help us to be mindful of your presence, this Advent and always, that we might be your witnesses to everyone we meet, and especially to those we teach.
All	Give us the gift of waiting, loving God. Help us to keep alert, to stand firm in our faith, to be courageous and strong. Let all that we do be done in love.
Leader	Take a few minutes now to pray silently for the gift of Advent waiting and for any particular needs you have in your ministry as a catechist.
	Allow five minutes or so. If your setting permits, invite catechists to move wherever in the room they can comfortably pray. After five minutes, invite everyone to gather around your prayer table.
Leader	I invite you to come forward now to take a copy of this prayer. Pray it often during Advent as a reminder that God is already present.
	As catechists come forward, say to each:. "_____, may you receive the gift of waiting."
Leader	Be with us now and always, loving God, and please bless and watch over those we teach. We ask this in Jesus' name.
All	Amen.

9

Jesus Is Our Light

To Prepare

On your prayer table place a lighted candle, a bible (open to John 1:1–5), and cut out paper candles, one for each catechist, with these words on them: "May Jesus always light your way." If possible, lower or turn out any other lights in the room.

Leader   Before the world was created, the Word already existed; the Word was with God, the same as God. From the very beginning, the Word was with God. Through him God made all things; not one thing in all creation was made without him. The Word has life in himself, and this life brought life to us. The light shines in the darkness and the darkness has never put it out.

After a brief pause, invite catechists to reflect in silence on the following questions.

Reader One   How do you feel when you are alone in the dark? (pause)

Reader Two   Look at the light of the candle. How do you feel about this light? (pause)

Reader One   Consider for a moment that John calls Jesus "light," the light that shines in our darkness. Close your eyes and think of Jesus in this way. (pause)

Reader Two   John also says the darkness has never put out Jesus' light. How do you feel knowing that Jesus is always with you, always "light" in your darkness? (pause)

Leader   In the Western world the liturgical season of Advent comes at the darkest time of the year. But our faith assures us that Jesus is the light of the world, a light that darkness has not overcome. This is our joy and our consolation, and this is the message of Christmas. This is the message we are called to teach.

Reader Three	Jesus, light of the world, help us to *believe* in the gift of your presence.
All	Please give us the light of faith.
Reader Four	Jesus, light of the world, help us to *trust* in the gift of your presence.
All	Please give us the light of trust.
Reader Five	Jesus, light of the world, help us to *love* you, present in one another and in those we teach.
All	Please give us the light of love.
Leader	Jesus, help us as we now prepare our minds and hearts for Advent. Teach us and our children to hope for your coming and to believe in your light.
	Give each participant a candle as you say the following blessing: "May Jesus, the light of the world, dispel your darkness. May he light your way during Advent." After each individual blessing all may respond as below.
All	May you always live in the light.

10

We Wait with Patience

Leader Every year during Advent we teach children that this is the time to prepare for the coming of Jesus. Advent is a time of waiting, symbolic waiting, because Jesus was born over 2000 years ago. At Christmastime, we *commemorate* the birth of the savior, but still we wait.

Questioner Is our Advent waiting really only symbolic? Is it really over at Christmas? Aren't we also preparing during this time to better respond to Jesus in our daily lives—here and now?

Leader Jesus is indeed already among us. Even during Advent, as we symbolically wait, hope, and prepare, Jesus is with us. Perhaps our real Advent challenge is to teach our children how to relate to the Jesus who has already come—and not only to a babe in the manger. Sometimes I am afraid we're teaching our children to be like the people in the following Russian fable.

Reader One "A great and important person was soon to visit the village. The people met in the village square and made decisions about decorations and food and entertainment. They formed committees and soon began making lavish preparations.

Reader Two "In the midst of these preparations, the great visitor arrived. The people were devastated; they weren't ready. A delegation went to the village gate to ask the visitor to go elsewhere for a few days, since the preparations were not complete. Sadly the visitor turned away."

Leader Aren't we Christians like this? We use the four weeks of Advent to make frantic preparations for Christmas Day. It is the day itself we want, not the coming of Jesus into our daily lives.

Questioner	We say with our mouths "Jesus is the reason for the season," but what we actually celebrate is our materialism. But still, I must ask: How can our Advent waiting be merely symbolic? Aren't we in fact waiting for Jesus to come at the end of time?
Leader	Yes, we are waiting for that, too. Part of the tension of our Christian faith is to relate to Jesus in the present, though he lived in the past and will come again in glory. Even those who knew Jesus "in the flesh" must have been puzzled when he said: "I will be with you always." It seems clear from the letters of Paul that he, too, pondered this. He had only known Jesus "in spirit," but he looked forward to meeting him at a future time. In a message to his young disciple, Timothy, he put it this way:
Reader Three	"In the presence of God and of Christ Jesus, who is coming to judge the living and the dead, I charge you to teach the word *now*, to stay with this task, whether convenient or inconvenient—correcting, reproving, appealing—constantly teaching and never losing patience.
Reader Four	"Be steady and self-possessed; put up with hardship, perform your work as a teacher. Fulfill your ministry until the day when the Lord will reward you—and not only you—but all who have eagerly awaited his coming. " The Word of the Lord.
All	Thanks be to God.
Leader	Let us accept Paul's message to Timothy as our challenge, too, especially as we begin preparations for Advent and Christmas. Let us now pray in silence to the Holy Spirit, the Spirit of Jesus, to guide and enlighten us as we attempt to share the presence of Jesus with those we teach.
	Allow five minutes for silent prayer.
Leader	Please come forward now for a closing blessing.
	As you give each person a verse card say these words: "_____, *stay with your teaching task, whether convenient or inconvenient,* *and never lose patience."*
	Close by offering one another a Sign of Peace.

11

We Receive the Light

Leader   The light of Christ our savior shines out in the darkness, and the darkness is not able to overcome it.

All   Thanks be to God.

Leader   Jesus, you are the light of the world. Teach us to live in your light that you might scatter the darkness of our fears, our sorrows, our faults and our failings. Help us to believe that you are present with us now, offering us your light. Teach us to live in your light.

Reader One   A reading from the prophet Isaiah:
"The people that walked in darkness have seen a great light; on those who live in a land of deep shadow, a light has shone.

Reader Two   "O God, your light has made our gladness greater, it has made our joy increase; we rejoice in your presence as people rejoice at harvest time."
The Word of the Lord.

All   Thanks be to God.

Leader   We are God's people; together we have walked in darkness, and together we have seen a great light. This candle lighting the way for us is a sign of the presence of the risen Christ who dwells among us. Let us reflect, each in his or her own heart, on this presence.

If you have small candles for each person, light these now from the larger candle. Invite all to sit, and as they hold their flickering candles—or watch the flickering of the larger candle—spend five minutes or so in silent prayer and reflection.

Reader Three   Let us pray. That we might walk in the light and guide those we teach away from the darkness of sin toward the light that comes from God, let us pray to the Lord…

All   Jesus, teach us to live in your light.

Reader Four   That we might recognize and overcome the darkness in ourselves and help those we teach to do the same, let us pray to the Lord…

All   Jesus, teach us to live in your light.

Reader Five   That we might have the faith and courage to believe that Jesus, the light of the world, is always with us, ever guiding us, let us pray to the Lord…

All   Jesus, teach us to live in your light.

Reader Six   That each of us might overcome the particular "darkness" that keeps us from effectively proclaiming the gospel, let us pray to the Lord…

All   Jesus, teach us to live in your light.

Leader   Let us now extinguish our candles, resolving to continue in the belief that Jesus, our light, is among us always.

Conclude this service by inviting participants to offer one another the following blessing: "_____, may you live in the light of the Lord." The recipient answers: "Amen."

We Are Called to Serve

To Prepare

Place on your prayer table a candle (an Advent candle or a Christ candle) and a bible, open to Matthew 25:31–42. After participants have gathered, darken the room and light the candle.

Leader We are gathered here in the presence of God and one another to reflect on the meaning of Christmas. We do this as much by how we prepare as by our actual celebration on December 25. Let us resolve now in the company of God and one another to use the weeks of Advent to pray, reflect, and act as God would have us do.

Allow five minutes or so for silent prayer and reflection.

Reader One A reading from the Gospel of Matthew:
"When the son of Man comes in his splendor…all the nations will be gathered before him and he will separate people like a shepherd separating sheep from goats. He will place the sheep on his right hand, and the goats on his left.

Reader Two "He will say to those on the right: 'Come, take your inheritance…for I was hungry and you gave me food. I was thirsty and you gave me drink. I was lonely and you made me welcome. I was naked and you clothed me. I was ill and you came and looked after me. I was in prison and you came to see me.'

Reader Three "Then the people will say: 'But when did we see *you* hungry or thirsty or lonely or ill? When did we see *you* in prison?' And he will answer: 'I assure you, whatever you did for the humblest of my sisters and brothers, you did for me.'"

Leader Perhaps the real question is: can we truly celebrate Christmas as followers of Christ if we are not living the message of the one we follow?

Reader Three The best preparation for Christmas might be to resolve to "live" the gospel in our daily lives. Jesus tells us what this means in the reading we have just heard. We will be judged on our willingness to love and serve others. This is the sole criterion he offers. And then he tells us what it will mean if we ignore the gospel message.

Reader Four	"Then he will say to those on his left: 'Get out of my presence and go into the eternal fire. When I was hungry you gave me nothing to eat. When I was thirsty you gave me nothing to drink. When I was lonely you never made me welcome. When I was naked you did not offer to clothe me. When I was sick and in prison, you never cared about me.'
Reader Five	"And they will ask him: 'When did we see *you* hungry or thirsty or lonely or ill? When did we see *you* in prison?' And he will answer: 'I assure you, whatever you failed to do for the humblest of my sisters and brothers, you failed to do for me.'" The Word of the Lord.
All	Thanks be to God.
Leader	As we pray and reflect in preparation for the birth of Jesus, let us also resolve to live this gospel message. Let us ask ourselves: How can we better serve the needs of our sisters and brothers? How can we share this challenge with those we teach?
	Again, allow time for silent reflection—two minutes or so.
Leader	Jesus, you have already come among us. You are already our Emmanuel. But we are weak and slow to understand.
Right Side	Help us to discover what your Word asks of us.
Left Side	Open our minds and hearts to the needs of others.
All	Teach us how to open the minds and hearts of our children and youth.
Leader	We need your help, Jesus. We believe that you are with us, but we need your guidance to prepare for and celebrate your birth according to your Word. We ask this in the name of the Father, and of the Son, and of the Holy Spirit.
All	Amen.

We Are the Church

To Prepare

On your prayer table place a bible (open to Philippians 4:4–7) a lighted candle, and any symbols of Advent that seem appropriate for your group. Also have an empty container and small slips of paper, at least two for each participant.

Leader   God of all seasons, God of light and darkness, guide us as we reflect on our call to be "church" for our world. Help us to announce the presence of Jesus in all that we do, especially our teaching, and to be signs of your love and justice. Give us the courage to face the darkness as well as the light. Teach us to wait patiently. Amen.

Reader One   "Rejoice in the Lord always, again I say rejoice!

Reader Two   "Let your patience and self-control be visible to everyone.

Reader Three   "The Lord is near. Have no anxiety, but offer prayers of thanksgiving and let your petitions be made known to God.

Reader Four   "And may the peace that surpasses all understanding guard your hearts and minds in Christ Jesus."

Reader One   The Word of the Lord.

All   Thanks be to God.

Leader   Paul's instructions to the Christians in Philippi offer a brief summary of how we ought to be as "church," the body of Christ in our time and place. He exhorts us to (read the following slowly and reflectively):
•always rejoice,
•have patience and self-control,
•pray in thanksgiving,
•offer all our petitions to God, and
•carry in our hearts the ultimate sign of faith, the peace that surpasses all understanding.

I invite you now to consider which of these five gifts you possess most fully and write it on a slip of paper. Consider, too, which gift you are most in need of and also write that on a slip of paper. When you have finished writing, place your unsigned slips in the container on our prayer table.

Allow five minutes for silent meditation. When all have placed their papers in the container, continue.

Leader As we await the new birth of Jesus in our hearts and minds, let us offer thanksgiving and make our petitions known to God.

Reader Two Loving God, thank you for moments of joy. Teach us to *always* rejoice in your presence…

All The Lord is near!

Reader Three Thank you for the gift of patience, loving God; strengthen us to practice it…

All The Lord is near!

Reader Four Thank you for *always* being with us, loving God. Remind us to pray often…

All The Lord is near!

Reader One Loving God, thank you for the gift of peace; let it guard our minds and hearts in Christ Jesus…

All The Lord is near!

Leader (while holding up the container on the prayer table):
Loving God, teach us how to be faith-filled members of your church. We offer you our gifts and our needs, our thanksgiving and our petitions. Make of us a holy people that we might fittingly serve your children. We ask these things in Jesus' name.

All Amen.

14

We Listen to God

<table>
<tr><td></td><td>To Prepare
Place a candle and a bible (open to Psalm 139) on your prayer table. Invite catechists to gather around it.</td></tr>
</table>

Leader	Glory be to the Father, and to the Son, and to the Holy Spirit…
All	…as it was in the beginning, is now, and ever shall be, world without end. Amen.
Reader One	"My God, you know the whole of my journey…and you walk in front of me and behind me; sometimes I feel your hand resting on my shoulder. Your loving presence seems too good to be true.
Reader Two	"You always understand my spirit; you know each cell of my body. You have been with me in all that I have done, and will be with me until the end.
Reader One	"If I flew on the wings of the dawn, if I sailed to the far limits of the sea, your hand would still be upon me, guiding me and holding me safe.
Reader Two	"Your plan is wonderful, more than I can grasp. I rest in you in faith and live in your love." The Word of the Lord.
All	Thanks be to God.
Leader	If we can believe the words of the psalmist, God is always with us. This includes the times that we teach and prepare to teach. God is always guiding us. Our problem is that we do not *attend* to the presence of God. We do not ask for God's help and listen to God's response. I invite you now to silently reflect on this. Is it true in your life? When and how do you attend to God? How might you improve?
	Allow three to five minutes for personal reflection.
Reader Three	When we pray, we lift our minds and hearts to God, who is already

with us. We do not have to search the wings of dawn or the limits of the sea, we simply have to look into our own hearts and quietly listen.

Reader Four   Why is it so hard for us to do this? Why is it so difficult to sit still, to be quiet, to attend to God? Is it really that we don't have time? Or are we afraid of what God might ask?

Reader Five   Let us resolve during this Lent—and all year through—to begin anew to listen to God. Let us allow God to lead us, to speak to us, and to change us. And let us introduce those we teach to this God who dwells within them.

Leader   God, you know the whole of our journey.

All   You walk in front of us and behind us.

Leader   Sometimes we feel your hand resting on our shoulders.

All   Your loving presence seems too good to be true.

Leader   You always understand us.

All   You know each cell of our bodies.

Leader   You have been with us in all that we have done.

All   And you will be with us until the end.

Leader   If we fly on the wings of the dawn, or sail to the far limits of the sea.

All   Your hand will still be upon us, guiding us and holding us safe.

Leader   Your plan is wonderful, more than we can grasp.

All   We rest in you in faith and live in your love.

Leader   Gracious God, please open our hearts and minds and strengthen our faith that we might experience your presence. Help us to share this faith with those we teach. We ask these things in Jesus' name.

All   Amen.

We Walk with Jesus

To Prepare

Have construction paper and markers available for each participant. Have taped lenten music ready to play. Place on the prayer table an open bible, a lighted candle, and a crucifix. Optional: prepare a poster or banner that reads: Come Follow Me, and hang or place this in clear view.

When everyone has arrived, announce that before praying, you will spend time preparing the 15 visuals to be used during the prayer service. You will need one visual for each of the 14 Stations of the Cross, plus one for the Resurrection. These visuals should be: numbered, simple, and symbolic of Lent. Individual catechists might each prepare one, or catechists can work in small groups. What to depict and how to proceed should be entirely up to the participants.

Allow ten minutes or so for the group to come up with ideas. Then play the taped lenten music as the visuals are actually being prepared. When all 15 are ready, place them around the room, so that there will literally be 15 stations or stops during the service.

Leader	When Jesus issued the invitation "Come follow me," he was not speaking to disembodied spirits. His followers were real people, who were called to follow him with heart, mind, body, and spirit. We will now reflect together on how we, as Christians, as catechists, might better follow Jesus this Lent. Let us begin.
Reader One	(move to visual 1) Pilate, a man who did not know Jesus personally, unjustly passed judgment on him. • How often in our teaching ministry do we make unjust judgments about those we teach?
Reader Two	(move to visual 2) The instrument of his death was cruelly thrust on Jesus' shoulders. •What heavy burdens does our ministry place on us? (silent reflection)
Reader One	(move to visual 3) Jesus fell to the ground in full view of the crowd. •Are there times when we "fall" in full view of children, parents, co-catechists?
Reader Two	(move to visual 4) Mary stood by helplessly as Jesus passed by; to

all but her eyes he was a failure.

•How often do those we teach disappoint us or cause us sorrow?

Reader One (move to visual 5) Simon the Cyrene reluctantly helped Jesus carry the cross.

•How often have we come to our teaching ministry reluctantly?

Reader Two (move to visual 6) Veronica risked personal danger to comfort and cleanse Jesus.

•Are there times we take risks to offer the comforting words of faith?

Reader One (move to visual 7) Jesus fell again beneath the weight of the cross.

•How many times have we "fallen down on the job" through our own fault?

Reader Two (move to visual 8) The women of Jerusalem wept for Jesus, but he rebuked them.

•How many times in our teaching ministry have we "wept" with self-pity?

Reader One (move to visual 9) Though Jesus fell for the third time, he struggled to get up again.

•How often have we been tempted to give up, by not making the extra effort our ministry requires?

Reader Two (move to visual 10) Jesus was stripped of everything, even his clothing.

•How willing are we to give "everything" when God makes demands on us?

Reader One (move to visual 11) The soldiers nailed Jesus, now stripped and abandoned, to the cross.

•Do we rely on the strength that comes from God when our ministry is discouraging or painful?

Reader Two (move to visual 12) Jesus, after speaking words of forgiveness, died on the cross.

•Do we pray words of blessing and forgiveness for those we teach?

Reader One (move to visual 13) The body of Jesus was placed in Mary's arms, his mission apparently over.

•How often do we give up on those we teach because they are *apparently* hopeless?

Reader Two (move to visual 14) Jesus is placed in Joseph of Arimathea's tomb.

> •When everything goes wrong, how strong is our faith in the resurrection?

Reader One   (move to visual 15) After three days, Jesus was raised to new life.
•Do we let setbacks and discouragement rule us—or are we alleluia people?

Leader   Jesus, our risen one, help us to use this lenten time to ponder the mysteries of our faith and to deepen our belief in the resurrection. We ask these things for ourselves and for those we teach.

All   Amen.

Invite 15 participants to go around the room, one at a time, to pick up the symbols. As each is solemnly brought forward and placed on the prayer table, all recite the following together:

All   Jesus, teach us how to follow you. Teach us how to teach.

Continue until all 15 symbols are on the table.

16

We Celebrate God's Forgiveness

> **To Prepare**
> Place on your prayer table a lighted candle, a bible (open to Colossians 3:5–15), and any symbols that represent Lent for you and your catechists.

Leader   During Lent, we contemplate and celebrate the great gift of God's forgiveness. Whatever our sins, our faults and failings, God offers us forgiveness.

Reader One   While we believe in God's forgiveness, we also acknowledge our need to change and grow, especially in our role as catechists, to become more like Jesus in our thinking, our decisions, and our actions.

Reader Two   And so let us acknowledge the presence of Christ and celebrate God's forgiveness, but let us also resolve anew to change and grow, in a word, to put on Christ.

Leader   God, our God, you are always forgiving. You love us beyond our comprehension, and in so loving you call us forward, out of our familiar patterns, into new life in Jesus Christ, your son.

Reader Three   This is how St. Paul put it:
"This is God's plan, to share with you a rich and glorious secret. The secret is this: Christ is in you! This means that you share the glory of God. So, preach Christ to everyone, with all possible wisdom, in order to bring each one into God's presence as a mature Christian.

Reader Four   "To this end, you should get rid of anger, uncontrolled passion, and hateful feelings. No insults or obscene talk should ever come from your lips. Don't lie to one another because you have now put on Christ.

Reader Five   "You are the beloved people of God. So put on compassion, kindness, humility, gentleness, and patience. Be helpful to one another and forgive one another. In fact, you must forgive one another in the same way that God forgives you.

Reader One   "And to all these things add love, which binds everything together

in perfect unity. And always be thankful; Christ's message in all its richness lives in your hearts."
The Word of the Lord.

All   Thanks be to God.

Left Side   Come to us, Jesus, our risen savior. Help us to remember that you are always with us, offering us forgiveness and unconditional love.

Right Side   Help us to believe in you, to follow you, and to proclaim your teaching faithfully.

Left Side   Come to us, Jesus, our risen savior. Help us to remember that God has given us a rich and glorious secret.

Right Side   Help us to be worthy of this trust and to proclaim it with joy.

Pause for three minutes of silent prayer.

Leader   In a particular way, during the weeks of Lent as we await the glorious celebration of Easter, let us resolve to pray always, to live simpler lives, and to reach out to those in need, especially those we teach. Let us ask God's forgiveness if we have failed in these ways…

All   Have mercy on us, forgiving God, this Lent and always. Amen.

We Are Called to Service

To Prepare

Place on your prayer table a candle, a bible (open to John 13:4–9), a white towel, a basin or bowl, and as many small white cloths—4 x 4" squares—as there are members of the group.)

Leader   Jesus, our risen savior, you are present here through your Holy Spirit. Open our minds and hearts to hear your word, this Lent and always.

Reader One   "Jesus rose from the supper table, took off his outer clothes, picked up a towel and fastened it round his waist. Then he poured water into the basin and began to wash the disciples' feet and to dry them with the towel around his waist.

Reader Two   "In this manner he came before Simon Peter, who said to him: 'You must never wash my feet!' Jesus answered, 'Unless you let me wash you, you cannot share my lot.' 'Then, please,' Peter countered, 'wash my hands and face as well!'"
The Word of the Lord.

All   Thanks be to God.

Left Side   Here we are, Lord, your followers, your friends. Your message to us is that as you have done, so we must do. How are we to serve your children? How are we to wash their feet?

Reader Three   When we take time to prepare lessons…when we enter a room full of lively children…when we proclaim our Word and share our faith…this is washing their feet.

Right Side   Here we are, Lord, your followers, your friends. Your message to us is that as you have done, so we must do. How are we to serve your children? How are we to wash their feet?

Reader Four   When we come to catechist meetings, or scripture study sessions, when we attend a catechetical conference or a workshop, when we volunteer for paraliturgies and field trips, this is washing their feet.

All Here we are, Lord, your followers, your friends. Your message to us is that as you have done, so we must do. How are we to serve your children? How are we to wash their feet?

Leader I invite you now to reflect on this question in silence. What is the answer closest to your own heart?

Allow five minutes or so for this.

Leader Here we are, Lord, your followers, your friends. Your message to us is that as you have done, so we must do. How are we to serve your children? How are we to wash their feet?

Ask volunteers to "pray aloud" ways that they might better serve the children they teach. You can begin the process in this way: "Jesus, help us to be more patient (more creative, to add more humor, etc.)."

When all have named something, take the white cloths from the prayer table. Facing your catechists present these "towels" (one at a time) as you say: "_____, receive this towel as a symbol of your lenten service."

After each presentation, all can respond: "Amen."

Leader Jesus, you have given us an example; you have shown us how you want us to serve. We want to throw in our lot with you, to follow you. Please give us the courage we need to offer service to your children and to one another.

All Amen.

18

Jesus Prays for Us

> **To Prepare**
> Have paper and pencils available for each participant. Place on your prayer table a bible (open to John 17:6–21), a lighted candle, and a bowl or other container.

Leader　　Blessed be God, and blessed be all that God has created. Blessed be God's children, who have been given over to our care.

Reader One　At the Last Supper, Jesus poured out his heart in prayer. One of the key elements of his prayer was concern for those who would be proclaiming his Word. He prayed in this way:

Reader Two　"Father, I revealed your name to those whom you have given me…and they have kept your word. Now they know that everything you gave me is from you, because the words you gave me I have given to them, and they accepted them and truly understand that I come from you. I pray for them…Holy Father, keep them in your name, so that they may be one just as we are.

Reader Three　"Consecrate them in the truth. Your word is truth. As you sent me into the world, so I send them into the world…And I pray not only for them, but for those who will believe in me through their words, so that they may all be one, as you, Father, are in me and I in you, that they also may be one in us, that the world may believe that you sent me."
The Word of the Lord.

All　　Thanks be to God.

Reader Four　It's hard for us to imagine that Jesus was thinking of us as he was about to suffer and die, but indeed he was. He obviously considered our work as proclaimers very important.

Leader　　We are now about to embark on a lenten journey of faith, accompanied by those we teach. We have been called to offer them the truth that Jesus spoke of in his prayer. This can be a challenging, even fearsome task. But we don't go forward alone. Jesus prayed to the Father to *accept* us—as Jesus is accepted—that we might be one with God. And so we "go with God."

Hand out the paper and pencils and invite each participant to first reflect about, and then write down, his or her goals for the lenten journey. Allow five minutes or so for this.

Leader   I invite you to come forward now, one by one, and place your "goals" in the container on our prayer table. As you do so, say these words, aloud or in your heart: Jesus, I will place my trust in you this Lent.

When all have placed their papers in the bowl, hold it high as the closing prayer is said.

Reader Five   Jesus, you prayed for us at your Last Supper, and we believe that you continue to pray for us now. We ask you to be with us as we begin our lenten journey. Help us to work toward our goals and give us your courage, your peace, and your love that we might worthily proclaim your Word to those we teach. We ask this in the name of the Father, and of the Son, and of the Holy Spirit.

All   Amen.

19

We Ask for God's Mercy

To Prepare	

To Prepare
Place the following objects on your prayer table: a white candle, a bowl of water, and a bible (open to Psalm 145). If this service is done in church, you may want to substitute the baptismal font for the bowl of water.

Leader	"Great is our God and worthy of all praise. Together let us praise God who offers us gracious compassion and who is slow to anger and full of love for us.
Reader One	"Gracious God, you are faithful in all your words, and holy in all your works. You lift up all who are falling and raise up all who are bowed down.
Reader Two	"The eyes of all look hopefully to you, and you give them bread in due season. You open your hand and satisfy the desire of every living thing.
Reader Three	"Gracious God, you are just in all your ways and loving in all your works. You are near to all who call upon you, to all who call upon you sincerely.
Reader Four	"You fulfill the desire of those who fear you, you hear their cry and save them. You watch over all who love you." The Word of the Lord.
All	Thanks be to God.
Leader	We acknowledge that we are in need of God's compassion and forgiving love. We are teachers and proclaimers, called to be models for those we serve, and yet we know how weak we are. Together let us ask God's forgiveness for the times we have failed to be models of compassion and love.
Reader One	For the times we have forgotten that it is God's Word we proclaim and not our own, Lord, have mercy.
All	Lord, have mercy.

Reader Two	For the times we have failed to be compassionate and forgiving toward those we teach, Christ, have mercy.
All	Christ, have mercy.
Reader Three	For the times we have not been just in all our ways, or loving in all our works, Lord, have mercy.
All	Lord, have mercy.
Reader Four	For all the times we have failed to give witness to our God, who is slow to anger and full of love, we ask forgiveness and the grace to change.
All	Lord, have mercy; Christ, have mercy; Lord, have mercy.
Leader	I invite you now to spend a few moments in quiet reflection.
	Allow five minutes or so for this.
Leader	Gracious God, you lift up those who are falling and you raise up all who are bowed down. You are near to all who call upon you, to all who call upon you sincerely.
All	We have acknowledged our sins and you have forgiven us. You have lifted us up that we might be worthy witnesses. We ask you to wash us clean in your waters of forgiveness.
Leader	(extending hands over the bowl of water). Yahweh, our God, bless this water and let it remind us that you offer us gracious compassion and love. We ask this in the name of your son, Jesus Christ, who lives and reigns with you forever and ever.
All	Amen.
	Invite participants to come forward one at a time to bless themselves with the water. When all have finished, invite them to offer this greeting to one another: "May God bless you with compassion and love."

20

We Pray with the Spirit

To Prepare
Place the following objects on your prayer table: a white candle, a bible (open to Romans 8:14–27), and paper and pencils for all participants.

Leader Our God is a God of mystery, but also a God of love. We praise you, our God, and we believe in your presence among us. We believe, too, in your love for us, which has been revealed to us through your Word.

Reader One "Those who are led by the Spirit of God are children of God and they can cry out, 'Abba, Father!' The Spirit bears witness with our spirit that we are children of God.

Reader Two "In the same way, the Spirit, too, comes to the aid of our weakness; for we do not know how to pray as we ought. The Spirit intercedes for us with inexpressible groanings. And the one who searches our hearts knows that it is the intention of the Spirit that we do God's will." The Word of the Lord.

All Thanks be to God.

Reader Three Guided by the Holy Spirit, let us cry out, "Abba, Father!"

All Abba, Father!

Reader Four Holy Spirit you bear witness with our spirits that we are children of God. Teach us to pray, "Abba, Father."

All Abba, Father!

Reader Five You come to our aid in prayer, for we don't pray as we ought. You intercede for us with cries and groans. Teach us to pray, "Abba, Father!"

All	Abba, Father!
Reader Six	The God of mystery and love, who searches our hearts, knows that you cry out for us and that you want us to do God's will. Teach us to pray with confidence, "Abba, Father!"
All	Abba, Father!
Leader	I invite you now to spend a few moments in quiet reflection. Know in your hearts that even if prayer words or thoughts don't come easily, the Holy Spirit is praying within you and knows all that you need.
	Allow five minutes for silent prayer. Invite participants to use the paper and pencils on the prayer table if they feel inclined to write out their thoughts and prayers.
Leader	Let us now pray together for guidance in our role as catechists and also for those we teach. That we might be examples to our children as we pray with them and for them, let us pray to the Lord…
All	Lord, hear our prayer.
Leader	That we might grow in faith, especially in our belief that the Holy Spirit prays in us and for us, let us pray to the Lord…
All	Lord, hear our prayer.
	Invite participants to now offer spontaneous prayers.
Leader	Our God is a God of mystery, but also a God of love. We praise you, our God, and we believe in your presence among us. We believe, too, in your love for us, which has been revealed to us through your Word.
All	Increase our faith that we may join the Spirit who cries out within us, "Abba, Father!" We ask these things through Jesus Christ, Our Lord, who lives and reigns with you and the Holy Spirit, forever and ever. Amen.

We Are Victorious with Jesus

> **To Prepare**
> Place a candle and a bible (open to Revelation 2:17) on your prayer table. If possible, have available a small white stone for each catechist.

Leader   Gracious God, you know us and you love us. You know all of the joys, pains, successes, and struggles we have experienced so far this year as your teachers and catechists. Guide us as we now reflect on our response to your call.

Reader One   "Those who have ears to hear, let them listen to what the Spirit is saying. To those who prove victorious, I will give the hidden manna and a white stone—a stone with a new name written on it, known only to the person who receives it."
The Word of the Lord.

All   Thanks be to God.

Leader   This brief reading serves as an invitation to us to reflect on our role as catechists. It invites us in particular to decide if we have proved "victorious." What does it mean to be victorious as catechists? I invite you to close your eyes and prayerfully ponder the following questions:

•When those you teach are inattentive or disruptive, how do you react? Do you give up or do you keep trying to win their attention?…(pause)

•What do you do when those you teach are bored and indifferent about God's Word and God's presence? Do you accept defeat or do you keep trying to rouse them?…(pause)

•What keeps you going from class to class? Is it realization that this commitment will soon be over, or is it believing that God can and does work through you—sometimes in mysterious ways?…(pause)

•By what standard do you measure victory? By everything going well, by the reaction of your learners, by how good you feel about a lesson, or none of the above?…(pause)

•What do you think God means by victory in your role as catechist?

	What do you think God expects of you?…(pause)
Leader	Most of us tend to expect far too much of ourselves and at the same time rely far too little on God, whose presence we are proclaiming. Perhaps the ultimate definition of victory depends on how well we have focused on God. If we have proclaimed God's presence, in season and out, no matter how successful our lessons have been, we have proved ourselves "victorious." I invite you now to listen to another brief reading from Revelation (Rev. 7:12), one that calls itself the "song" that those who are victorious sing.
Reader Two	"Amen! Let us give to our God praise and glory, wisdom, thanksgiving, and honor. Power and might belong to our God forever and ever. Amen!" The Word of the Lord.
All	Thanks be to God.
Reader Three	May our work as catechists always give God praise and glory.
All	Amen.
Reader Four	May we always share with those we teach the gift of God's wisdom.
All	Amen.
Reader Five	May we, together with those we teach, give God thanksgiving and honor.
All	Amen.
Reader Six	May we, through our teaching, acknowledge God's power and might forever and ever.
All	Amen.
Leader	I invite each of you to come forward now to receive a symbolic reminder of your call to "listen to the Spirit." *As each comes forward to receive a stone, say: "_____, may you always prove victorious." When all have received their stones, recite the closing prayer.*
Leader	Gracious God, you are with us always. Teach us to rely on your wisdom and strength. We ask these things in Jesus' name.
All	Amen.

22

We Live in the Holy Spirit

> **To Prepare**
> On your prayer table place a jug or pitcher of water with a small "finger bowl" beside it, and assemble as many outward signs of the sacraments as you wish, for example: a white cloth, a baptismal candle, unconsecrated eucharistic bread, a wedding ring, the oil of anointing, a priest's stole. Place a bible at the center of the table (open to 1 Corinthians 2:13–16).

Leader   There are many times in our lives as Christians that we celebrate sacred events. These public rituals are celebrated in the presence of a faith community. Most notable among these sacred events are the seven sacraments. In our ministry as catechists we are often the ones who teach children, youth, and adults about the sacraments. We are the ones who prepare them for the ceremonies in which they will publicly receive the sacraments.

Reader One   This experience is often frustrating because we know that those we teach view these sacred events as "one-time only" experiences, which are isolated from their daily relationships, activities, and decisions. In his letter to the Corinthians, Paul offers insights about why this might be so. He explains why it is so difficult for people to grasp the meaning of sacred events.

Reader Two   "We do not speak in words taught by human wisdom, but in words taught by the Spirit of Jesus. This is especially true when we are trying to explain spiritual truths (like the sacraments). Those who do not have the Spirit cannot understand what we are saying, and they cannot receive the (sacramental) gifts that come from God's Spirit.

Reader Three   "Such people really don't understand the gifts of God; in fact these gifts are nonsense to them, because the value of God's (sacramental) gifts can only be judged on a spiritual basis—and these people are not living daily in the Spirit. Those who do live in the Spirit are able to judge the value of everything, because they have put on the mind of Christ."
The Word of the Lord.

All   Thanks be to God.

Leader	Before we can ask those we teach to hear the Spirit of Jesus, we must reflect on our own ability to hear "words taught by the Spirit of Jesus." Let us now prayerfully reflect together.
Reader Four	Do we allow ourselves to be taught by the Spirit of Jesus, that we might better understand spiritual events—like the sacraments? (pause for reflection)
Reader Five	Are we ourselves aware of receiving spiritual gifts from God's Spirit? If yes, what are these gifts? (pause for reflection)
Reader Six	Do we ourselves live in the Spirit daily? In other words, does our relationship with Jesus directly influence our daily relationships, activities, and decisions? (pause for reflection)
Reader Seven	Have we ourselves "put on the mind of Christ"? In what ways? (pause for reflection)
Leader	Let us pray. Holy Spirit, Spirit of God and Spirit of Jesus, open our eyes and our hearts that we might acknowledge your presence and welcome you.
All	Open our ears to hear the words of wisdom you are ready to speak to us.
Leader	Holy Spirit, we have welcomed you and listened to you. Teach us how to proclaim the great gift of your presence to those we teach. We ask this through Jesus Christ, our teacher, friend, and brother.
All	Amen.

Go now to the prayer table and pour a small amount of water from the jug into the finger bowl. Then turn to the person nearest you, and, dipping your finger into the water, make the Sign of the Cross on that person's forehead saying: "Go forth and proclaim the gift of God's presence." That person should answer: "Amen." Then take the bowl, turn to the next person and repeat the blessing, and so on until all are blessed. The last person to be blessed should come forward to sign and bless you. When you respond "Amen," the ritual is concluded.

23

We Are Spirit People

To Prepare

Place the following objects on a prayer table at the front of the room: a white candle, a bible (open to Acts 1:8), a basin or bowl of water, and a white cloth (if possible, one of the baptismal cloths your parish uses). Beforehand, prepare for each participant a small verse card that reads, "I have called you by name." Also beforehand, hang in a visible place a sign or banner that reads, "God calls us by name."

Leader	After his resurrection (before he was taken up to heaven), Jesus spoke these words to his followers.
Reader One	"You will receive power when the Holy Spirit comes upon you; then you are to be my witnesses in Jerusalem, throughout Judea and Samaria, yes, even to the ends of the earth."
Leader	When we were baptized, we received this promised Spirit, the Holy Spirit, the Spirit of Jesus himself. At that moment we were one with all those who witness to the presence of Jesus in our world.
Reader Two	At the moment of our baptism, we (or our parents or godparents for us) publicly expressed our belief that we belong to God. We accepted the waters of baptism as a sign of the way we would be living, the Christian way.
Leader	At that moment we received a lighted candle as a sign that we would let our light shine in the darkness—the light of our faith in Jesus.
Reader Three	At that moment, too, we were given a new garment to wear as a sign that we would imitate Jesus, or as Paul expressed it, we promised to "put on Christ" throughout our lives.
Leader	At that moment of our baptism, God called each of us by name to be a child of God, to be one with Jesus in the family of faith called church.
Reader Four	When we bring a child to this family of faith, we often forget that we, too, were once brought forward. We, too, were washed in the waters of forgiveness. We, too, once pledged our faith and received our call to be witnesses to Jesus. We, too, were called by name to be

lights to our world. Let us now pray together as we recall our baptismal gifts.

Right Side	We have been baptized in the name of the Father…
Left Side	God, you have called us by name. We belong to you.
Right Side	We have been baptized in the name of the Son…
Left Side	God, you have given us your light. We will let it shine.
Right Side	We have been baptized in the name of the Holy Spirit…
Left Side	God, you have robed us in glory. We will "put on Christ."
Right Side	We have been baptized in the name of the Father, and of the Son, and of the Holy Spirit…
Left Side	God, you have given us new life in Christ. We will follow Jesus.
All	We will be witnesses, as Jesus commanded us to be. We will proclaim your name, even to the ends of the earth.
Leader	We have been made one family through the waters of our baptism. Let us now pray together…
All	Our Father, who art in heaven, hallowed be your name; your kingdom come, your will be done, on earth as it is in heaven. Give us this day our daily bread, and forgive us our trespasses, as we forgive those who trespass against us. And lead us not into temptation, but deliver us from evil. Amen.

Now light the white candle and invite participants to stand in a circle around your prayer table.

Leader	God has given us signs and symbols to remind us •that we are known and loved individually, by name, •that we belong to a family of faith, •that we were washed in the waters of forgiveness, •that we are to be witnesses of Jesus. I invite each of you now to come forward to receive a sign of your baptismal pledge. (As each person is handed his or her card, say the following:) "_____, God has called you by name."
All	(After each participant receives his or her card:) Thanks be to God.

24

We Welcome God's Gifts

To Prepare

Place on your table a bible (open to Acts 2:1–4), a candle, a bowl (or other container), and any symbols of the Holy Spirit that seem appropriate. Have available slips of paper and pencils for all participants.

Leader   May the Holy Spirit be with you and pour out upon you unimaginable gifts. May the Holy Spirit bless you and strengthen you. I ask these things in Jesus' name.

All   Amen.

Leader   All praise to you, Holy Spirit. You were revealed to the followers of Jesus in a mighty wind, and you touched them with tongues of fire. Come, fill our hearts with your fire and wind as we now share God's Word.

Reader One   "When the time for Pentecost was fulfilled, they were all in one place together. And suddenly there came from the sky a noise like a strong driving wind, and it filled the whole house.

Reader Two   "Then there appeared to them tongues as of fire, which parted and came to rest on each one of them. And they were all filled with the Holy Spirit and began to speak in different tongues, as the Spirit enabled them to proclaim."
The Word of the Lord.

All   Thanks be to God.

Leader   Each of us hears these words from a different perspective. Some of us would probably like the excitement of fire, wind, and noise. Others would be terrified by it. Some of us are risk takers and some of us are not. But we all have needs.

Reader Three   So it was with the disciples. They had different needs and reactions, but the Holy Spirit came to them all. The Spirit strengthened them and gave them the courage to use their own particular gifts more fully.

Leader	I invite you now to spend quiet time reflecting on the scene just described in scripture and your reaction to it. If the Holy Spirit came among us right now, how would you feel and what special gift would you ask for? After thinking about this, write your request on a slip of paper and place it in the container on the prayer table.
	Pause for five minutes of silent prayer.
Reader Four	Holy Spirit, give us your gift of wisdom that we might know what is most important in life.
All	Holy Spirit, gift us with wisdom.
Reader Five	Holy Spirit, give us your gift of understanding that we might genuinely care for one another.
All	Holy Spirit, gift us with understanding.
Reader Six	Holy Spirit, give us your gift of knowledge that we might know right from wrong.
All	Holy Spirit, gift us with knowledge.
Reader Seven	Holy Spirit, give us your gift of fortitude that we might courageously live our faith.
All	Holy Spirit, gift us with fortitude.
Reader Eight	Holy Spirit, counsel us that we might make unselfish decisions for ourselves and others.
All	Holy Spirit, gift us with counsel.
Reader Nine	Holy Spirit, give us the gifts of piety and fear of the Lord that we might reverence and love God in all that we do.
All	Holy Spirit, gift us with piety and reverence.
	Appoint a reader to pray each of the following lines, and then do the appropriate movement yourself and ask catechists to follow your lead. Ask the reader to allow sufficient time between each line so that the movements can be done reverently.
	Holy Spirit, you gift us in so many ways. Once again we come before you confident that you are listening. *(Fold your hands.)*

We are ordinary people and we are needy.
(Open your hands and cup them.)

How can we be the ones called to proclaim your presence?
(Extend hands and arms outward.)

We can't lead others unless you lead us.
(Lift both arms above your head.)

We acknowledge your greatness and your goodness.
(Bow your head deeply.)

And we want to lead our children to you.
(Hold outstretched arms in front of your body.)

Show us how to be signs of God's presence in all that we do. Help us to follow Jesus.
(Make a wide arch with your hands and arms.)

We ask these things in the name of the Father, and of the Son, and of the Holy Spirit. Amen.
(Make a Sign of the Cross and once again fold your hands.)

25

We Celebrate the Church

> **To Prepare**
>
> Place on your table a lighted candle, a copy of the documents of Vatican II, and a large sign or poster that reads: "We are proclaimers; we are catechists."
>
> Note that this service is based on images of the church described in *Lumen Gentium* (the Constitution on the Church), a key document of Vatican II.

Leader	God, our loving parent, we are gathered here today to reflect on your presence in the church. You have appointed us to serve your church as proclaimers of the faith, as catechists. Send us your Holy Spirit that we might receive the gifts of wisdom and understanding to help us proclaim your kingdom on earth. May your Spirit guide us as we now reflect on our mission and on the images of your church.
Reader One	The church is a sheepfold whose one and necessary door is Christ. She is a flock of which God promised to be the shepherd. Although guided by human shepherds, her sheep are nevertheless ceaselessly led and nourished by Christ himself...
Leader	Come, Holy Spirit, teach us to follow Jesus in our role as shepherds of the church.
All	Come, Holy Spirit, come.
Reader Two	The church is a tract of land to be cultivated, the field of God. The church has been cultivated by the heavenly vinedresser as a choice vineyard. The true vine is Christ who gives life and fruitfulness to the branches, that is, to us. Through the church we abide in Christ, without whom we can do nothing.
Leader	Come, Holy Spirit, teach us to follow Jesus, and to carefully cultivate your vineyard, the church.
All	Come, Holy Spirit, come.
Reader Three	The church has often been called the edifice of God. This edifice has many names: the house of God in which God's family dwells; the household of God in the Spirit; the dwelling place of God among people; and especially, the holy temple...

Leader	Come, Holy Spirit, teach us to follow Jesus by building up the church, the dwelling place of God, the holy temple.
All	Come, Holy Spirit, come.
Reader Four	The church is called our mother. She is described as the spotless spouse of the spotless Lamb. She it was whom Christ loved and delivered himself up for that he might sanctify her…He filled her with heavenly gifts for all eternity, in order that we might know the love of God and of Christ for us, a love that surpasses all knowledge.
Leader	Come, Holy Spirit, teach us to follow Jesus in love and service to our mother, the church.
All	Come, Holy Spirit, come.
Leader	Let us now pray to the Holy Spirit in the silence of our hearts. Let us ask for the gifts we need to carry out our ministry as proclaimers, as catechists in the church.
	Allow three minutes for silent prayer.
Leader	Please respond: Holy Spirit, hear our prayer.
	That we might be wise shepherds, who love and care for the children and youth in our parish, let us pray to the Lord…
All	Holy Spirit, hear our prayer.
Leader	That we might cultivate the field of God with patience and diligence, let us pray to the Lord…
All	Holy Spirit, hear our prayer.
Leader	That we might honor and cherish our mother, the church, in imitation of Jesus, let us pray to the Lord…
All	Holy Spirit, hear our prayer.
Leader	Let us go now, guided by the Holy Spirit, to reflect on our role as catechists and on our call to serve the church.
All	Thanks be to God.
	Invite all present to share the Sign of Peace before leaving.

26

We See and We Hear

To Prepare

Before this meeting, ask catechists—in person or by mail—to bring to the meeting a small object that symbolizes God's presence for them. As they arrive, place these objects on a central prayer table on which there is a lit candle and a bible (open to Matthew 13:10–17).

Leader   The Lord be with you.

All   And also with you.

Leader   We are gathered here to reflect on the great mystery of God's abiding presence. May God open our minds and hearts to this gift.

Reader One   "The disciples said to Jesus, 'Why do you use parables when you teach?' Jesus answered, 'The knowledge of the secrets of the kingdom of heaven have been given to *you*, but not to everyone…I use parables because people look, but do not see, and they listen, but do not hear or understand.

Reader Two   'Remember what the prophet Isaiah said: "This people will listen and listen, but not understand. They will look and look, but not see, because their minds are dull, and they have stopped up their ears and have closed their eyes. Otherwise, their eyes would see, their ears would hear, their minds would understand, and they would turn to me, and I would heal them."

Reader Three   'As for you,' Jesus continued, 'how fortunate you are! Your eyes see and your ears hear. I assure you that many prophets and many of God's people wanted very much to see, but they could not, and to hear what you hear, but they did not.'"
The Word of the Lord.

All   Thanks be to God.

Reader Four   What is it that Jesus wants us to see? Is it that God's kingdom is already among us? And that there are signs pointing to it all around us?

Reader Five	What is it that Jesus wants us to hear? Is it the sounds of life in our created world, the voices of our needy brothers and sisters, the Word solemnly proclaimed at our liturgies?
Reader Six	How fortunate we are. Jesus tells us that our signs and sacraments symbolize something beyond themselves. They point us to the presence of God, the kingdom of God.
All	How fortunate we are. Our eyes *do* see and our ears *do* hear the signs and sacraments of God's presence.
Leader	I invite you to reflect silently about what God is saying to you through the symbols you have placed on our prayer table.
	Allow three minutes or so, and then ask catechists to come forward in turn, and pick up their symbol from the prayer table. Facing the group, and holding high the symbol, each should announce: "This is a sign of God's presence." All can respond: "Amen." When all have held up their objects, hold up the bible and announce: "This, too, is a sign of God's presence." End with the following prayer.
Leader	Jesus, guide us as we continue to study the signs of your presence among us. Open our hearts and minds to whatever it is you want us to see and hear more clearly this day. Amen.

27

We Need God's Gifts

> **To Prepare**
> On your prayer table place a bible (open to 1 Kings 3:7–12), and a candle.

Leader	Grace and peace be yours from our gracious God and from our Lord Jesus Christ!
All	May they also be yours.
Leader	Let us pray. Lord God, you have called us to serve you in the midst of your people, especially your young people. We pray that we may teach with understanding hearts and know what is right. Trusting in your guidance, we reach out to you with our talents but also our weaknesses. Strengthen us that we may proclaim your Word. For this we pray in the name of our Lord Jesus Christ.
All	Amen.
Reader One	When Solomon was still a young man, he acknowledged in his prayer that he needed God's guidance. He humbly admitted that he lacked the skills of a leader.
Reader Two	He told God that he felt overwhelmed by the number of people under his care, and so he prayed…
Reader Three	"Give me an understanding heart, great God, to govern your people. Help me to discern what is right or wrong and to choose between good and evil."
Reader Four	It pleased God that Solomon asked for spiritual gifts rather than material ones, and so God answered Solomon's prayer in this way…
Reader Five	"Here and now I will do what you ask. I give you a heart wise and shrewd, as no one has had before and no one will have after you."
Leader	Loving God, our spiritual needs are many. Give us please the gifts we need to be wise and understanding catechists.

Now pray spontaneous prayers that apply to your own group in particular. Invite catechists to add their prayers to yours.

Leader   Gathering our prayers into one, let us together pray:

All   Our Father in heaven, may your name be held holy. Your kingdom come, your will be done, on earth as in heaven. Give us today our daily bread, and forgive us our debts, as we have forgiven those who are in debt to us. And do not put us to the test, but save us from the evil one. For yours is the Kingdom, and the power, and the glory, now and forever. Amen.

Leader   We have heard the call of God to serve in the midst of the young people in our parish. But let us remember that God was pleased when Solomon asked only for an "understanding heart." From that gift all others flowed. So, let us pray together now for the gift of an understanding heart for ourselves.

Ask each person to pray aloud the following words for the person to his or her right, until every person present has been mentioned by name: "Lord, please give _____ the gift of an understanding heart."

Leader   Lord, you are a generous God. Gift us with wisdom and understanding so that our catechetical ministry may accomplish the work of Jesus Christ. Let your spirit fill our lives; let your love make us compassionate catechists. We ask this in the name of our Lord Jesus Christ, who taught us to be servants of all.

All   Amen.

28

We Praise God Always

To Prepare

Have available paper and pencils for all participants. On the prayer table place a candle, a bible (open to Psalm 148), and an empty container.

Reader One   (Very dramatically): Alleluia! Let the heavens praise God. Praise God, heavenly heights; praise God, sun and moon; praise God, all you shining stars.

Reader Two   All created things, praise the name of God at whose command you were created. Let Earth praise God: sea monsters and all deep waters, fire and hail, snow and mist, storm winds that fulfill God's command, mountains and hills, orchards and forests, praise God.

Reader Three   Wild beasts and all tame animals, all you snakes and birds, all of you, all created things, praise God, for God's name alone is exalted above heaven and earth. Alleluia! Alleluia!

Reader Four   All created things are dependent on Earth's changes. We call these changes seasons. Indeed, the seasons determine whether ice and snow or orchards and forests praise God. Nature's changes can be violent or they can be subtle. They can alter our way of life or barely affect it. They can offer us beauty and grandeur or struggle and challenge. In all these ways nature reveals to us the power and presence of God.

Leader   Let us enter into the mystery of the seasons as we reflect on the following questions. (Pause briefly after each question.)

•Do you change with the seasons? In what ways? …
•What is your favorite season? In what ways does it "speak" to you? …
•What is your least favorite season? What struggles does it present? …
•What do the seasons tell you about God? …
•How might you share the wonder of the seasons with those you teach? …

I invite you now to write down your strongest impression about the season we are now enjoying—as a prayer. You can express wonder, serenity, anger, struggle, joy, sorrow, whatever emotion this season evokes in you. When you have completed your prayer, place it in the container on the prayer table.

Allow sufficient time for this. When all have placed their papers in the container, continue as below.

Reader Five   God, our beloved creator, you have given us the seasons. May they praise you, and may we praise you through them. Accept our summer praise: for sunshine, for lakes and all bodies of water, for crops growing in the fields, for all your summer gifts, we thank you.

All   For all your summer gifts, we thank you.

Reader Six   Accept our autumn praise: for changing colors, for frost, for acorns falling, for crops harvested, for all your autumn gifts, we thank you.

All   For all your autumn gifts, we thank you.

Reader Seven   Accept our winter praise: for cold and ice, for snow and wind, for the brown earth awaiting rebirth, for all your winter gifts, we thank you.

All   For all your winter gifts, we thank you.

Reader Eight   Accept our spring praise: for budding flowers and new grass, for warm days and cool nights, for the rebirth that gives witness to resurrection, for all your spring gifts, we thank you.

All   For all your spring gifts, we thank you. Amen.

Leader   (As you hold up the container) God of all seasons, accept our praise and our pleading, our expressions of joy and our words of sorrow. Just as Mother Earth changes and renews, so let us change and renew, especially in our role as proclaimers of your Word. With all created things, we praise your name. Amen.

All   Amen. Alleluia.

29

We Journey with the Saints

> **To Prepare**
> Place on your prayer table a bible (open to Revelation 7:9–10) and a candle. Light the candle and then invite catechists to close their eyes and breathe deeply, slowly inhaling and exhaling five times. Explain that this is a way to breathe in God's presence and put away distractions and noise. Then spend three minutes in silence.

Leader   As we gather to reflect on our role as catechists, let us recall some of the church's great teachers who have gone before us.

Reader One   Albert the Great was a lifelong scholar who was interested in many things. He reminds us that we are all *learners* who have to listen more closely to God in our lives.

All   Lord Jesus Christ, son of the living God, keep us faithful to your teaching, and never let us be parted from you. Help us to be lifelong learners, always open to new possibilities.

Reader Two   Clare of Assisi, though born wealthy, chose to live in poverty. Throughout her life she shared whatever she had with the poor. She and her followers shared their spiritual gifts and a life of prayer.

All   Lord Jesus Christ, son of the living God, keep us faithful to your teaching, and never let us be parted from you. Help us to share our gifts with one another and especially with those we teach.

Reader Three   Pope Gregory the Great was a talented spiritual leader and he was widely admired for his intelligence and devotion to the church. He called himself the "servant of the servants of God."

All   Lord Jesus Christ, son of the living God, keep us faithful to your teaching, and never let us be parted from you. Help us to gladly serve your children through our teaching and our love and care.

Reader Four   Perpetua was a young wife and mother who lived in the third century, a time of persecution for Christians. She was imprisoned and eventually put to death because she would not renounce her faith.

All   Lord Jesus Christ, son of the living God, keep us faithful to your teaching, and never let us be parted from you. Help us to value our faith and to share it willingly with those we teach.

Leader   I invite you to reflect silently for a few moments about your role as a catechist. Call upon your own personal heroes and heroines of the faith. Ask for their prayers and guidance on your efforts, and ask them to show you the way to Jesus in all that you do, especially your teaching.

Reader One   A reading from the Book of Revelation.

"After that I saw a huge number, impossible to count, of people from every nation, race, tribe, and language; they were standing in front of the throne and in front of the Lamb, dressed in white robes and holding palms in their hands. They shouted aloud, 'Victory to our God, who sits on the throne, and to the Lamb…forever and ever. Amen.'"

The Word of the Lord.

All   Thanks be to God.

Leader   Lord Jesus Christ, son of the living God, keep us faithful to your teaching, and never let us be parted from you. Help us to join our voices with your angels and saints, who down through the ages have prayed, "Victory to our God and to the Lamb forever and ever."

All   Praise and glory and wisdom and thanksgiving and honor and power and strength to our God, forever and ever. Amen.

30

We Rejoice in God's Works

> **To Prepare**
>
> Place on your table a bible (open to Philippians 1:3–10) a list of the names of all your catechists, aides, and office helpers, a list of names of the children and teenagers in your program, and a candle. Beforehand, invite catechists to bring to this end-of-year service samples of class work or any other tangible signs of their ministry as catechists. Light the candle and invite catechists to close their eyes and breathe deeply, slowly inhaling and exhaling five times. Explain that this is a way to breathe in God's presence and put away distractions and noise. Then spend three minutes in silence.

Leader   May the blessings of our good God be with each of you.

All   And also with you.

Leader   Loving God, as we come to the end of our teaching year, I thank you for all your gifts and in particular for these coworkers of mine, without whom your work could not have been done. I join my words to those of Paul in his letter to the Philippians.

Reader One   "I give thanks to my God at every remembrance of you, praying always with joy in my every prayer for you, because of your partnership for the gospel from the first day until now.

Reader Two   "I am confident of this, that the one who began a good work in you will continue to complete it until the day of Jesus Christ. It is right that I should think this way about all of you, because I hold you in my heart as partners with me in grace…

Reader Three   "This is my prayer: that your love may increase ever more and more in knowledge and every kind of perception, to discern what is of value, so that you may be pure and blameless on the day of Christ's coming."
The Word of the Lord.

All   Thanks be to God.

Leader   All of us have received great gifts this year, among them, love and support from one another, cooperation from parents, lessons that went very well, and the light of God reflected in the eyes of our children. I invite you now to name particular moments or experiences for which you are grateful.

You may want to begin by holding up your list of catechists, aides, and office helpers, and the list of children's names, while praying: "For all our parish catechists and other volunteers, and for every child in our classes…" If catechists have brought items to share, have them hold these up as they voice their prayers.

All   (after each statement): We rejoice in your good works, loving God.

Leader   We have all received gifts this year, and many of us also experienced setbacks, some of our own making and some not. I invite you to reflect silently about any problems you may have had this year, or about any of the ways that you may have fallen short as a catechist. Place all of these in God's hands and know that God blesses and forgives you unconditionally.

Allow three minutes or so for this.

Leader   We rejoice in your good works, loving God, and we thank you for your patience with our shortcomings…Thank you for calling us to share the gospel message with our children and teenagers. We pray these things in the name of the Father and of the Son and of the Holy Spirit.

All   Amen.

Of Related Interest ...

Prayer Services for Parish Meetings
Debra Hintz

This book of 40 prayer services gives leaders the necessary encouragement and means to begin small or large group sessions in a prayerful manner.
0-89622-170-9, 96 pp, $9.95 (order B-07)

Prayer Services for Religious Educators
Gwen Costello

32 prayer services that beautifully address areas such as liturgical feasts, contemporary concerns, and other faith topics useful to prayer leaders. The services are brief, yet deeply inspiring.
0-89622-390-6, 82 pp, $9.95 (order W-93)

Psalm Services for Group Prayer
William Cleary

The ancient psalms of David form the basis for half the prayer services in this book. The other half features original psalms by the author.
0-89622-526-7, 96 pp, $9.95 (order B-58)

Psalm Services for Parish Meetings
William Cleary

Cleary offers prayer services for otherwise ordinary meeting times, using the scriptural book of psalms and poetic psalms he has written.
0-89622-510-0, 96 pp, $9.95 (order W-35)

Weekly Prayer Services for Parish Meetings
Lectionary-Based for Year A
Marliss Rogers, editor

Helps parish groups open their meetings in a more prayerful, reflective manner. Services are organized around readings for each Sunday of Year A.
0-89622-646-8, 120 pp, $12.95 (order M-34)

Weekly Prayer Services for Parish Meetings
Year B
693-X, 120 pp, $12.95 (order M-75)

Weekly Prayer Services for Parish Meetings
Year C
0-89622-599-2, 112 pp, $12.95 (order M-09)

Available at religious bookstores or from:

XXIII **TWENTY-THIRD PUBLICATIONS**
P.O. Box 180 • Mystic, CT 06355 • 1-800-321-0411